SUPERSTARS
OF SPORTS

LeBRON JAMES

BASKETBALL SUPERSTAR

BY TYLER OMOTH

CAPSTONE PRESS
a capstone imprint

Blazers Books are published by Capstone Press,
1710 Roe Crest Drive, North Mankato, Minnesota 56003
www.mycapstone.com

Library of Congress Cataloging-in-Publication Data
Names: Omoth, Tyler author.
Title: LeBron James : basketball superstar / by Tyler Omoth.
Description: North Mankato, Minnesota : An imprint of Capstone Press, [2019]
   | Series: Blazers. Superstars of Sports | Includes index. | Audience:
   Ages: 9-14.
Identifiers: LCCN 2018002677 (print) | LCCN 2018004344 (ebook) | ISBN
   9781543525120 (eBook PDF) | ISBN 9781543525045 (hardcover) | ISBN
   9781543525083 (paperback)
Subjects: LCSH: James, LeBron—Juvenile literature. | Basketball
   players—United States—Biography--Juvenile literature. | Cleveland
   Cavaliers (Basketball team)—History—Juvenile literature. | African
   American basketball players—Biography—Juvenile literature.
Classification: LCC GV884.J36 (ebook) | LCC GV884.J36 O66 2019 (print) | DDC
   796.323092 [B]—dc23
LC record available at https://lccn.loc.gov/2018002677

Editorial Credits
Carrie Braulick Sheely, editor; Kyle Grenz, designer; Eric Gohl, media researcher;
Tori Abraham, production specialist

Photo Credits
Newscom: ABACAUSA.COM/Bill Ingram, 20, Icon SMI/Bob Falcetti, 8, MCT/Hector Gabino, 25, Reuters/Gary A. Vasquez, 23, Reuters/Lucy Nicholson, 16, Reuters/Peter Morgan, 13, Reuters/Ron Kuntz, 6, 11, 14, 17, USA Today Sports/Greg M. Cooper, 5, USA Today Sports/Jeremy Brevard, cover, USA Today Sports/Kelley L Cox, 22, USA Today Sports/Ken Blaze, 29, USA Today Sports/Kyle Terada, 26, WENN/Jeff Daly, 19

Design Elements: Shutterstock

Quote Sources
Page 9, "23 for 23: Little-known facts about LeBron James." 4 June 2015. ESPN.
http://www.espn.com/blog/cleveland-cavaliers/post/_/id/1028/23-for-23-little-known-facts-about-lebron-james
Page 14, "LeBron James Interview." 4 January 2004. InsideHoops.com. http://www.insidehoops.com/lebron-james-interview-010403.shtml
Pages 21, "Dwyane Wade on LeBron, MJ."14 October 2016. NBA. http://www.nba.com/bulls/gameday/dwyane-wade-lebron-mj
Pages 23 & 28, "LeBron James Named Unanimous Finals MVP after Cavs' Game 7 win." 20 June 2016. ESPN. http://www.espn.com/nba/playoffs/2016/story/_/id/16351029/lebron-james-cleveland-cavaliers-named-unanimous-nba-finals-mvp

Printed and bound in the United States of America.
PA017

TABLE OF CONTENTS

CHAPTER 1

A STAR IN THE MAKING

In 2017 the Cleveland Cavaliers were battling the Boston Celtics in a **playoff** game. Cavaliers star LeBron James took a shot. Swish! He became the leading National Basketball Association (NBA) playoff scorer of all time.

playoff—a series of games played after the regular season to decide a championship

LeBron tries for a layup in the May 25, 2017, playoff game in which he became the NBA's all-time top playoff scorer.

LeBron James hugs his mother, Gloria, after a game in 2003.

LeBron James was born in Akron, Ohio, on December 30, 1984. His mother, Gloria, raised him. They often moved from place to place. In the fourth grade, LeBron started playing sports.

LeBron dribbles the ball during a basketball camp in 2001.

"I've always loved the success of my teammates more than myself. I've always been like that since I was a kid."

—LeBron James

Basketball and football were LeBron's favorite sports. He was very good at both. In middle school, his basketball skills stood out. He was a great scorer and passer.

LeBron played on his high school **varsity** team in 9th grade. He helped his team win three state championships. People noticed LeBron's talent. He was on the cover of *Sports Illustrated* magazine when he was in 11th grade.

varsity—the main team in a high school sport

FACT

LeBron was named Ohio's Mr. Basketball three times in high school. This award goes to the state's best high school basketball player of the year.

LeBron dunks the ball during a high school basketball game in 2003.

CHAPTER 2

WELCOME TO THE NBA

LeBron was known as the best basketball player in Ohio when he graduated from high school. In 2003 the NBA Cleveland Cavaliers **drafted** him. LeBron was the youngest player to open an NBA season as a **starter**. He was 18 years and 303 days old.

draft—to select a player to join a sports organization or team

starter—a player who appears in games when they start

LeBron stands with NBA Commissioner David Stern after being drafted on June 26, 2003.

LeBron dunks the ball to score in a game against the Denver Nuggets in 2003.

"I worked hard to get to the point where I'm at, and I'm happy to see the fans come out and watch us play."

—LeBron James

In his **rookie** season, LeBron led the Cavaliers in steals, scoring, and minutes played. Fans loved him. His great play earned him the NBA Rookie of the Year award.

rookie—a first-year player

FACT

On March 27, 2004, LeBron scored 41 points against the New Jersey Nets. He became the youngest player to score more than 40 points in an NBA game.

LeBron tries for a basket against the San Antonio Spurs in the 2007 NBA Finals.

LeBron quickly became a star. In the 2005-06 season, he led the Cavaliers to the playoffs. The next season, he led the team to its first-ever NBA Finals. The Cavaliers lost to the San Antonio Spurs.

In the 2004-05 season, LeBron made it on the Eastern Conference All-Star team. The Eastern Conference beat the Western Conference.

LeBron holds the NBA Eastern Conference Finals trophy after beating the Detroit Pistons in 2007.

17

CHAPTER 3

AWAY AND HOME AGAIN

In 2010 James was a **free agent**. Many teams wanted him. He chose to join his good friend, Dwyane Wade, in Miami with the Heat. Now two of the best NBA players were on the same team.

free agent—a player who can choose to play for any team

LeBron (right) and Dwyane Wade attend a party to welcome the Heat's newest team members in July 2010.

LeBron holds up the NBA championship trophy in 2012.

"Any team he's on is going to have the ability to go to the Finals. He's that great of a player."
—Dwyane Wade

The Heat became a huge success. The team made it to the NBA Finals four years in a row from 2011 to 2014. They won the NBA championship in 2012 and 2013.

FACT

LeBron played for the U.S. Olympic team in 2004, 2008, and 2012. The team won the gold medal in 2008 and 2012.

LeBron passes the ball during Game 7 of the 2016 NBA Finals.

After four years in Miami, LeBron decided it was time for a change. He returned to the Cleveland Cavaliers. He led the team to the Finals in 2015. The Cavaliers won the championship for the first time in 2016.

LeBron celebrates with teammates after the Cavaliers win the 2016 NBA championship.

"I came back to bring a championship to our city. I knew what I was capable of doing."

—LeBron James, after winning the 2016 NBA championship

CHAPTER 4

CAREER HIGHLIGHTS

LeBron has a career full of amazing highlights. During the 2008-09 season, he averaged 28.4 points per game. LeBron won his first NBA Most Valuable Player (MVP) award after the season.

FACT

LeBron also won the MVP award in 2010, 2012, and 2013.

LeBron holds the NBA MVP award in 2013.

LeBron shoots for a basket during the 2017 NBA Finals.

In the 2016-17 season LeBron led the Cavaliers to the NBA Finals again. They lost to the Golden State Warriors. But James broke a record. He became the player with the most **triple-doubles** in the Finals with nine.

FACT

In 2017 LeBron won an NBA citizenship award. LeBron has a *charity*. It helps youth find success in school in his hometown of Akron, Ohio.

triple-double—when a player earns a double-digit number in three areas during a game; these areas are points, rebounds, assists, steals, or blocked shots

charity—an organization that helps people in need

LeBron seems unstoppable. He has won three NBA championships and three Finals MVP awards. The future seems brighter than ever for the superstar.

"But the reason why he deserves this [the 2016 Finals MVP award] is because he has a great heart . . . and great things happen to great people."

—Tyronn Lue,
Cleveland Cavaliers coach

LeBron drives to the basket against Houston Rockets guard Chris Paul during a 2018 game.

TIMELINE

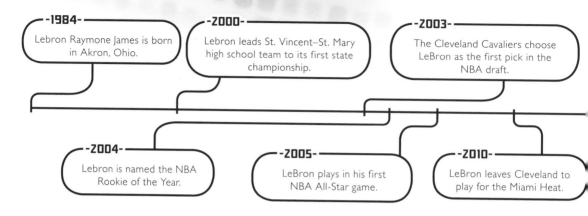

-1984-
Lebron Raymone James is born in Akron, Ohio.

-2000-
Lebron leads St. Vincent–St. Mary high school team to its first state championship.

-2003-
The Cleveland Cavaliers choose LeBron as the first pick in the NBA draft.

-2004-
Lebron is named the NBA Rookie of the Year.

-2005-
LeBron plays in his first NBA All-Star game.

-2010-
LeBron leaves Cleveland to play for the Miami Heat.

GLOSSARY

charity (CHAYR-uh-tee)—an organization that helps people in need

draft (DRAFT)—to select a player to join a sports organization or team

free agent (FREE AY-juhnt)—a player who can choose to play for any team

playoff (PLAY-ohf)—a series of games played after the regular season to decide a championship

rookie (RUK-ee)—a first-year player

starter (START-ur)—a player who appears in games when they start

triple-double (TRI-pul DUH-buhl)—when a player earns a double-digit number in three areas during a game; these areas are points, rebounds, assists, steals, or blocked shots

varsity (VAR-suh-tee)—the main team in a high school sport

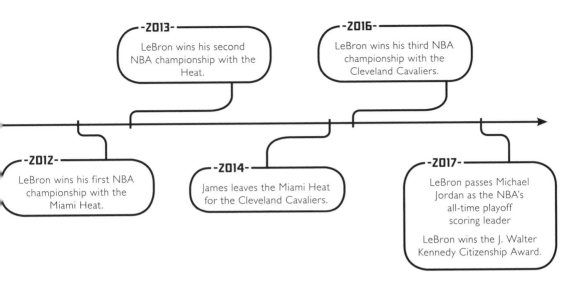

-2013-
LeBron wins his second NBA championship with the Heat.

-2016-
LeBron wins his third NBA championship with the Cleveland Cavaliers.

-2012-
LeBron wins his first NBA championship with the Miami Heat.

-2014-
James leaves the Miami Heat for the Cleveland Cavaliers.

-2017-
LeBron passes Michael Jordan as the NBA's all-time playoff scoring leader

LeBron wins the J. Walter Kennedy Citizenship Award.

READ MORE

Fishman, Jon M. *LeBron James.* Sports All-Stars. Minneapolis: Lerner Publications, 2018.

Gitlin, Marty. *LeBron James.* Basketball's Greatest Stars. Sportszone. New York: ABDO Publishing, 2017.

Storden, Thom. *Amazing Basketball Records.* Epic Sports Records. North Mankato, Minn.: Capstone Press, 2016.

INTERNET SITES

Use FactHound to find Internet sites related to this book.

Visit *www.facthound.com*

Just type in **9781543525045** and go.

 Check out projects, games and lots more at **www.capstonekids.com**

INDEX